Social Media Marketing

Build a Global Online Business in 2019,
Following The Marketing and Advertising
Network Secrets Strategy Guide Through
Instagram Facebook YouTube Twitter
Pinterest and LinkedIn

Joshua Reach

consent and can in no way be considered an endorsement from the trademark holder.

Table Of Contents

Introduction

The importance of going worldwide

If you are a small business owner that wants to remain competitive, you should consider opportunities for wider reach and production efficiency by doing business at the international level. Some niches are super-competitive in some regions but have tremendous growth opportunities in others. When you take your business global, you will have access to the marketplace with nearly 7 billion possible customers. This is a huge opportunity that you should not ignore.

One of the primary motives of going global is definitely to find new income streams. Sometimes there is too much competition at the local scene while other times businesses will saturate local markets. Growth opportunities may dry up, and this may trigger the need to grow a business beyond local borders. When a business successfully navigates its way into multiple national markets, it gains access to a broader customer base and generates new business. This leads to increased profits while minimizing costs.

Benefits of going global

1. Acquire more customers: While the US has about 4 percent of the global population, other nations much larger populations. For instance, China is at 19 percent while India has 17 percent of the world's population. Such large populations present opportunities for businesses to acquire more customers.

2. Increase revenue streams: By accessing new markets and acquiring new business opportunities and customers, a business will definitely increase its profits by creating new revenue streams.

3. Numerous other benefits: There are numerous other benefits available for you. These include market development, access to a larger talent pool, gain better margins, reducing dependence on the local market, and increased supplies and resources.

New 2019 Strategies that will Blow your Mind

Innovation in marketing in this era is essential. As a business owner, you need to keep yourself updated with some of the latest trends in marketing and advertising. There are quite a number of innovations that will be adapted in 2019 that will help to take your business to the next level.

Multichannel and Omni-channel marketing

The term Omni-channel originated around customers in order to describe marketing strategies that exist outside the travel and retail sectors. Omni simply means every kind, all, or the whole. Therefore, Omni-channel marketing refers to reaching out to customers and interacting with them across all possible communication channels. Even then, a focus should be placed on budgets so that only the most effective channels are selected.

As a business owner, getting online is no longer sufficient. You need to create a mobile responsive website. Such a website should also focus on speed and personalization. They should have a conversational user interface in order to create the ultimate customer experience.

Virtual and augmented reality: Businesses are now using mobile cameras in order to improve customer experience. Through both virtual reality and augmented reality, you can promote brand engagement and also make the pre-purchase decision much easier for your customers. The process will almost bring your products to life. Your customers will be able to make life much easier and better for your customers.

Artificial intelligence: Not many business owners or digital marketers make use of artificial intelligence. Yet it is a powerful tool that can be incorporated into your overall marketing strategy. Artificial intelligence is useful when it comes to improving user experience and simplifying data-based experiences.

These are just some of the emerging and existing techniques that are expected to become really big in 2019. If you are not applying them as part of your marketing strategy, then you may lose out.

Reasons why you must master marketing and advertising

Every small business starts by, among other things, focusing on getting their first customers. Online businesses often target online shoppers, especially those connected via Smartphones and other devices. Others rely on traditional forms of advertising like coupon mailers and print ads.

However, while these strategies of hoping customers will find business may work, it is advisable to adapt marketing strategies that will prove successful in the long run. For instance, digital marketing enables businesses of all sizes to reach huge online audiences in a measurable and cost-effective manner.

However, there are other benefits to learning digital marketing skills. There are numerous others as well. These include getting to interact with prospective clients and finding out exactly what they are searching for.

Digital marketing methods are much cheaper compared to traditional marketing means which enables you to reach a much larger audience at very low costs. You also get to track responses to your marketing efforts which in essence enables you to find out what is working and what you can improve on.

Marketing is a worthwhile activity

Marketing is viewed largely as an expense even though in essence it is an investment. It is a crucial activity especially when it comes to attracting the attention of new customers and prospective clients. You are able to develop services, and products demand and eventually turn prospective customers into actual customers.

Increased following easily translates into increased sales

As a business owner, you need to focus on increasing your presence on popular social media. This should be part of your larger digital marketing strategy. Most of your customers and prospective customers are on different social media. If you are not reaching out to them, then you are probably missing out on a huge opportunity.

The first thing you need to do is to expand your social media marketing channels. This means having a presence in as many media platforms as possible. The more popular ones include Twitter, Facebook, Instagram, YouTube, Pinterest, and LinkedIn among many others.

Since most of your customers are probably already on social media, you will easily be able to reach out them and encourage them to remain faithful to your brand. In the process, they will reach out to their followers and friends and introduce them to your brands.

If you have a multitude of followers, then they will reach out to even more friends and followers who will, in turn, introduce your products and brand. This way, you will be able to attract even more customers. Therefore, open accounts and business pages on as many social media platforms as possible in order to attract more customers and enjoy increased sales.

The technology used is organic in nature so no need to spend a lot of money

Organic technology serves a huge purpose within the broader marketing context; the requirements are quite high. For instance, you will need to make use of ranking hashtags and also create your own hashtags when you post your own content. Hashtags keep your content relevant and expose your brand to a much wider global audience.

You need to put high-quality content out there for others to see. It could be a website full of well written, relevant content that appeals to customers around the world. Take for instance the social media website Instagram. This specific social media is perfectly designed for lifestyle photos and images.

Organic technology provides traders with a huge opportunity to promote their brands and build their businesses. Getting the chance to communicate your brand's values and lifestyles is one of the benefits of digital marketing. All the social media platforms offer different solutions and opportunities to business owners. Therefore, as a business owner, you should not be surprised when you see consumers dance to music from your establishment.

Some of the other effects of organic social media include the fact that possibly only 3% to 4% of social media followers viewing a brand's products costs. Other benefits you can expect include communicating brand values, validating your brand, attracting new, very cool wait outside. There are also other benefits including influencer relationships, and so much more.

Organic serves a useful purpose when it comes to the broader marketing strategy. Before you embark into the river, you should take a look at your cash flow statements, bank, and so on. This way, you will be able to determine your budget and how much you can afford to spend. You should also consider paid adverts at this stage. This is because social media services such as Facebook have minimized the effects or benefits of organic search. Such platforms favor paid searches so you may need to combine the two. What is undisputed is the fact that paid advertising is a lot more effective when compared to natural, inorganic, advertising.

For traders, or business owners, or digital marketers, there is no better place to nurture influencer relationships that on social media. Anyone on the PR team or influencer marketers, you will largely rely on social media to connect with others.

You Should Give, Give, and Give First and then Start to TAKE

If you want to be successful on social media and the internet, then you need to attract a huge following and then build trust. This process is very effective if you know how to handle it. The first step is to come up with a social media marketing strategy. Once the strategy is in place, you should start informing your audience.

You should focus on growing your business and especially using social media. Provide useful and practical information to your readers. Let them come to trust you on matters that relate to your niche. Continue advising, researching, commenting and producing relevant content and share it with your followers. If you do this regularly, then you can expect to start receiving notifications and requests about your website.

All too often, business owners get on social media and begin asking customers to buy their products or use their services. This kind of approach is ill-advised primarily because your followers do not quite know you. No relationship has developed, and trust has not yet been established. Remember to first give and give some more, and the customers will eventually come calling.

Chapter 1: Building Loyal Customers

Just a couple of years ago, most businesses built customer relations based mostly on face-to-face interactions. However, this no longer applies especially today where plenty of transactions take place online. Even then relationships still have to be maintained. But its harder now to build trust and establish relationships because of problems such as cybercrime and online theft.

Customer loyalty

Customer loyalty is essential if you are to build and establish trust. However, since face to face interactions are no longer there, it is crucial for businesses to learn other ways of establishing loyalty and customer trust. Here are a couple of suggestions.

1. Connect with fans via social media: There is absolutely no doubt that your customers are on social media. Such platforms have been found to be the best places for interacting and communicating with your customers. A lot of consumers use social media to vet a business and see what others think about it. There are plenty of people who get onto social media in order to learn what people are saying about a particular product or service.

2. Provide online customer service: Another excellent way of building customer loyalty is providing customer services online. While most customers are online and not in stores, they still need to interact with and contact businesses. They also require assistance and advice from service providers and all others. Many customers seek help over the internet. If you can provide this service to your customers, then you will be assisting them immensely and strengthening existing relationships.

3. Come up with loyalty programs: One of the best ways of building customer loyalty is to develop and use loyalty programs. About 72% of Europeans and 76%American consumers prefer to shop at stores offering a loyalty program. Such programs are underutilized, yet they are extremely powerful. Customers love to feel wanted and appreciated. Such programs can be offered through free shipping, email coupons, contests, and loyalty points. When you offer such programs, you will have to honor them and not frustrate your customers.

4. Encourage customer reviews and prominently display them: Numerous consumers trust reviews and use them to make decisions about whether or not to purchase a product or use a service. Over 70% of global consumers rely on customer reviews in order to make purchasing decisions. Consumers trust reviews, especially from friends and family. Business owners can take advantage of this to boost the confidence of consumers. Make sure that you encourage customers to post reviews and share their positive experiences with others. When you encourage reviews, you show that you care about your customers' opinion. Building customer loyalty and trust is essential for any online business that wants to succeed. Customers have numerous options to choose from and will not engage with any businesses that do not make them feel valued. They will also not stay around when they feel their security is threatened. Therefore, take time and implement these simple solutions and customers will then come to trust you and become loyal and faithful to your brand.

Word of Mouth Marketing

One of the most powerful methods of marketing is through word of mouth. This is a powerful tool that works effectively even online. Word of mouth does not just catch people's attention but also gets them talking. Over 62% of consumers seek reviews on the internet before paying for a service or purchasing a product while more than 90% trust brand recommendations from family and friends.

With such numbers, it is crucial that you do not neglect this powerful marketing tool. The recommendations, ratings, and reviews of other customers are crucial when it comes to marketing and customer acquisition.

Think about the person who has a positive experience shopping online and then shares this experience on a platform such as Facebook or Twitter. This is a powerful and organic method of spreading information. Word of mouth marketing is basically a free form of advertising. It refers to personal experiences by customers that are shared with others through different channels.

Word of mouth marketing is also all about creating a buzz. As a brand, you want to gain a following, especially on the various social media. Remember that the more you interact with people then, the more your brand name gets known. This kind of effect is very similar to the snowball effect. Snowballs start small, but as they roll down a hill, they keep getting bigger and bigger.

Some of the tips you can use to implement word-of-mouth marketing include encouraging the use of user-generated content. This is content that is created and shared by consumers. It is usually honest and helps to build trust. It also makes the work of marketers much easier.

Whenever customers leave comments about their positive experiences at your online store, you need to ensure that these are shared across your social media. Testimonials by customers can be written on in video format. You can use platforms such as Crowd, Yelp, and others to share testimonials and comments. You should also seek to get product ratings on your website. Let your customers have the ability to rate or review certain services or products that you are selling.

How to Undertake a Product Launch

Brick and mortar establishments often launch products and services that involve the use of posters, decorating stores with posters, raffles, and giveaways.

The posters often feature the positives of the product or service while some sales representatives will coerce customers into buying the product at a discounted price. However, such tactics are unsuitable for online businesses. There are other more sophisticated marketing techniques that are suitable for online businesses. There are even frameworks that can guide you on how to launch a product online.

It is advisable to come up with a suitable launch strategy. This is because a launch can signal the beginning of a successful enterprise or a complete flop depending on planning and strategy.

The first step you need to make if you want to launch a product at your online store is to inform consumers about this product. A virtual launch needs to have a website that can take orders from customers and track sales of the products. You should offer discounted prices, offers, coupons and also a way of tracking performance.

Multi-channel approach

It is advisable to launch your products across multiple platforms. Just one platform is not enough. A successful approach should involve producing a viral video, creating teasers, and hosting blogs. It should also involve the use of social media platforms as most customers and followers of different brands are on these platforms. Therefore, when launching a product or a service, think about using multiple channels such as blogs, videos, social media, and so on.

Email marketing

Any well-designed product launch should also include email marketing as part of its strategy. While customers do not necessarily appreciate large amounts of email messages, emails offering samplers of a new product and promotional discounts are always welcome. This is basically an effective method of product promotion. Email marketing should also be used to offer the product at a special discount which may include incentives such as free shipping.

Social media campaigns

Social media is extremely effective when it comes to marketing and advertising your brand. Launching a new product is no different. You need to use a number of effective social media platforms as a launching pad for your products. Think about platforms such as Facebook fan pages, Twitter, and Instagram. Plenty of businesses are switching from print media advertising into the online media. Social media are excellent for most launch functions including interacting with customers, showcasing photos of the product, putting out videos and so on.

Cross-promotion

Another effective approach to product is launch is cross-promotion with other companies. You can find complementary vendors to work with who will undertake the cross-promotion. For example, a business producing skin care products can partner with a company that deals in bath product stores in order to provide amazing deals and discounted offers. In return, you will promote the bath products store and its products on your blogs and other platforms.

Other strategies that you should consider

1. Prelaunch giveaways: If you want your product to take off quickly then you should create an atmosphere of excitement and expectation. To be successful in this, you will need to come up with contests and even free giveaways. Identify a select group of individuals and let them have your product for free in exchange for promoting the product and getting the word out to others.

2. Enhance your organic visibility: Since you already have a website, you will need to optimize it for social media. A website that is optimized for search engines will give you a base of traffic that you can successfully use during the launch and afterward. To optimize your website, you will need to consider things such as a Meta description, keywords, and keyword phrases.

3. Create and share content: One of the most effective and reliable digital marketing strategies is the consistent creation of engaging, captivating, and informative content. This is something you need to keep doing in the medium to long run. You really should spend time creating a high-quality blog that contains useful information which adds value to your readers. The main purpose of the blog and the content you create is to provide your followers with an opportunity to share your content with their friends and followers. This will bring additional readers to your website, and the additional traffic will result in leads and eventually customers.

4. Consider remarketing: You need to have a strategy that understands it is not all about blindly impacting users but also about leading them through the conversion funnel. On your platform and social media profiles, you will have consumers at different stages of the purchase process. Not many consumers will be ready to join you after the initial contact. However, this should not mean that you should abandon them. Instead, stay with them and keep marketing your products to them. If you maintain contact, answer their questions and respond to their comments, you will eventually convert them into customers.

At the same time, you should still maintain contact with your current customers. You do not want them to go away. Therefore, keep in touch with your dedicated customers through social media, through newsletters, and through all other means. And remember to also let them know about any product launches that you plan.

5. Create a recommendation system: Another step that you can include as part of your product launch strategy is a recommendation system. As it is, word of mouth remains a superbly effective means of getting the word out about your products and brand. Most consumers tend to share the products they are using with their friends and family. When they share, you will probably receive more followers and possibly even new customers. Recommendations are definitely a welcome idea.

6. *Optimize your website's speeds:* There is basically nothing more frustrating than a slow website. When your visitors and customers are unable to load pages, make a purchase, or pay for products, they will definitely abandon your store and find another one. Fixing your website's speeds is a simple thing to do. Customers love websites that work at very fast speeds. A fast and fluid website enhances the customer experience as well as your brand perception. Talk to your website designer or service provider as they will be able to easily fix this for you.

7. *Establish a relationship with bloggers:* Digital marketing strategies are currently led by influencers. Many of them have their own blogs and command huge followings across different social media channels. This loyal following is willing and ready to listen to the influencer and follow their direction or recommendation. If you want the attention of influencers and bloggers, then you may have to pay them to promote your products and brand.

Alternatively, you could hold an event such as a launch and then send free samples to these influencers and bloggers. They will review the products and write reviews on their social media pages and blogs. However, they are very loyal to their followers and will never recommend something that they do not approve. Be sure to check out influencers in different niches before engaging their services. Try and identify which bloggers are best suited for your products and which ones are not. This way, you will be able to focus on a winner rather than take chances with one who stands little chance.

You can also nudge them to get the process started. This is easy as you can always offer an incentive. Simply create a system for recommendations where you reward any of your followers or customers who recommend your brand and products. People generally love free things so offer a free product or discounted offer if they share information about your product with their followers or friends and family.

Chapter 2: Where is your Audience Mostly?

As a business owner, it is crucial that you understand the different social media audience demographics. By doing this, you will be able to better select your social media channels and also improve your marketing.

Social media is absolutely important for any online business. However, there are numerous social media platforms out there. You have social networking websites such as Facebook, Twitter, Pinterest, LinkedIn, YouTube and many others. Each has its own kind of audience. For instance, users on platforms such as LinkedIn are a little different from those on Facebook and Instagram. This can make marketing a real challenge because of not knowing the most ideal platform to use.

Marketing on each social media is also pretty tough. It is a time-consuming exercise, yet the efforts may not necessarily pay off. Businesses and brands need to know which platforms are worth prioritizing so they can market themselves appropriately. This is why it is crucial to understand who is where and on what platforms are most of your customers. The knowledge will enhance your Facebook advertising and Instagram marketing techniques.

Do your research

It is well worth your time to research and find out who your right audience is and on what social media channels they are on. You need to think about the kind of audiences you need to reach on social media. You need to ask yourself a couple of questions. For instance, who is interested in your products and on what social media platforms are they? What can you do in order to appeal to a particular kind of audience?

Another question that you need to ask is what kind of platforms are your audiences on? First of all, you need to understand and appreciate the power of word of mouth marketing. This is a powerful marketing technique that works extremely well especially on social media. Your customers on social media are likely to talk about their experiences with a product or a service and then share this information with others. It is important to follow and connect with followers that are already connected to your target audience.

Demographics

Now your audiences and followers are not just a bunch of random people. They work in certain industries and sectors of the economy. Your audience lies within a certain age range and showcases a certain personality trait. Some love using social media while others are tech savvy. As a business owner and online marketing strategist, you need to do your research well and understand the demographics of your audience.

The best approach is to start by first segmenting your audience. This is easy if you start by creating follower profiles. Keep a record of this and use a spreadsheet to make things easier. Once you have the data that you need, keep the record and then analyze to find out what you come up with. It is possible that some unexpected outcome may result. Make sure that you keep updating this spreadsheet and keep improving your results.

Work with key influencers

Another step that you need to take is to identify influencers within your niche that you can work with. There are influencers on major social media sites with huge followings. They have dedicated followers who listen to them and follow their lead. Influencers generally stand out within a given community and others tend to listen to them. They include stakeholders within a given niche, thought leaders, journalists, and peers. Basically, they are individuals who challenge the ordinary and offer game-changing ideas and opinions.

Typical audiences

Some of your typical audiences that you will be searching for include the following individuals and groups of people;

- Your current customers or clients
- Potential customers or clients
- Associates of both current and potential clients or customers
- Editors and journalists
- Bloggers and influencers
- Affiliate businesses
- And thought leaders

Sometimes it is easy to pick these individuals and professionals out, but at other times you may need assistance. Fortunately, there are plenty of free monitoring tools that you can use. These tools can track down individuals mentioning keywords relevant to your business and niche.

Some of these tools include Board Reader, Social Mention, and Google Analytics. These will easily highlight the most crucial and most important voices in your niche area. Once these individuals have been profiled, you will need to track them down. Identifying them and then contacting them is a process that can take some time. You will have to find out which particular social media to use. So how will you do this? The solution will vary based upon your target audience.

Fortunately, you have access to information that can help to guide you through this process. There is insightful data available that shows you which demographics are found on which social media websites.

Facebook

Just about everyone is on Facebook. It is the world's largest social media platform, and most major brands and businesses have a presence here. As a business owner trying to promote your brand and gain new followers, you really have to be on this platform.

There are hundreds of millions of account holders on Facebook with more than 2 billion monthly users. Most users visit the website approximately every single day. Since Facebook is such a large website, it is safe to assume that most people have an account. However, there are certain clear trends that showcase the most active groups.

- Basically, women use Facebook a lot more than men. Over 83% of women are on Facebook while only 75% of men have accounts. This basically means you are able to reach both demographics even though you can reach more women than men.

- Most age groups are well represented on Facebook. This social media website represents just about all age demographics. Even then, most users or members are between the ages of 18 to 29. About 88% of young people in this age group are on Facebook. About 84% of individuals aged 30 to 49 have accounts, 72% of people aged between 50 and 64 years and about 62% of those aged over 65 years. It is only kids aged between 13 and 17 years who mostly prefer socializing on Snapchat.

- Most users on Facebook are college educated with a reasonable income. About 77% of people who claim to have attended or graduated college are on Facebook. This compares to about 56% of those who completed high school without attending college. Also, plenty of users on the platform earn at least $75,000 or more annually.

Twitter

Twitter is very popular when it comes to marketing. While it does not have a following as large as that of Facebook, it is very influential. It is said that at least 66% of users have discovered a brand or product on the site. Also, over 69% of users have made a purchase on the website based on content that they came across on the platform.

It is a platform where numerous brands should consider having a presence. Twitter has about 350 million users each month. These users visit the site almost every day. Basically, about 43% visit the website on a daily basis while about 24% visit the platform at least once a week.

Who is on Twitter? A lot of the demographics on Twitter are similar to those on Facebook. The main difference between the two platforms is that 21% of both women and men are on Twitter. Here are some more demographics about Twitter;

- *The most active demographics are young people:* Individuals aged between 18 and 29 are the most active on Twitter. Twitter users within this age bracket constitute about 36% of all users. Those between the ages of 30 to 49 years constitute about 22% followed by 18% of those aged between 50 and 64 years old. Only 6% of users are aged 65 years and above.

- *Most users have an advanced education and high incomes:* Just as with Facebook, a majority of users have high incomes with most users also claiming at least higher education qualifications.

- *There is a large international audience on the platform:* There is a huge presence of Twitter users who dwell outside the United States. More than 79% of users reside in places outside the USA with a majority of them based in Japan, Brazil, and Mexico. Twitter is, therefore, suitable for business owners seeking to sell to international buyers.

Instagram

The most popular social media website after Facebook has got to be Instagram. This social networking site lays a claim on 28% of the population. The site is used mainly to share photos, images, and videos rather than information. Even then the site attracts a huge number of users and has reportedly registered a huge number of engagements compared to almost all other platforms.

Instagram demographics

Instagram has more than 600 million users with active accounts. More than half of all users access their accounts at least every day while about 25% visit the website at least once each week.

A lot of the demographics are similar to those on Facebook and other platforms. Even then, there are plenty of young users on Instagram. They constitute the majority of users, and they spend a lot of time sharing visual content including videos and photos. These users are not just young but educated and trendy.

There are more female than male users on Instagram: This is the case not just on Instagram but on other platforms such as Facebook and Snapchat. However, the difference is larger here than elsewhere. More than 32% of women claim to have an Instagram account compared to only 23% of men.

Users are from all income brackets: Instagram users are from different income brackets. While there are some notable differences when it comes to percentages, the distribution is generally the same across the brackets. This is unlike the demographics on sites like Facebook where most users are middle- and high-income earners.

A lot of international users: Instagram boasts of a large international base of users. Just like Facebook and Twitter, there are plenty of users from around the globe. You can use Instagram as a perfect launching pad of selling to international customers.

After all, over 80% of Instagram users reside outside the United States.

LinkedIn

LinkedIn is a professional networking website. It is slightly different from other social networks in that it is more about professionals and businesses. However, it shares a number of demographic trends with other popular social networking websites. It is especially useful for businesses seeking to engage other businesses or B2B networking. Your advertising and marketing efforts will fare very well on this platform.

LinkedIn users

There are over 500 million users on LinkedIn. This mark was attained early in 2017. However, as this is a business network, users do not visit it as often as they should. At least when compared to other social networking sites. Only 18% of the 500 million users visit the website on a daily basis. About 31% visit only once a week. Most of all the other users claim to visit the site fewer times than that.

Demographics

It is easy to assume that LinkedIn is full of older people and less activity compared to other networking sites. However, this is not necessarily accurate. There are plenty of younger individuals on this platform. For instance, over 39% of LinkedIn users are aged between 18 and 29 years. Those aged between 30 and 49 years old constitute about 31% of users while 21% are aged between 50 and 64 years.

High levels of higher educated individuals: As expected, LinkedIn has a high number of highly educated individuals and professionals. More than half the members are college graduates. Those with some college education are at least 25%, and those with a high school education are about 9%.

High-income individuals: Members on LinkedIn are also well-paid individuals. Close to 50% of members earn at least $75,000 annually while only 23% earn less than $30,000.

Gender: There are more male users on this social network compared to all others. In fact, this is one of the very few social networking websites with more men than women. However, the difference is not that large. Twenty-eight percent of men have accounts on LinkedIn while only 23% of women have active profiles on the website.

Pinterest

The social networking site Pinterest is now considered among the major social media websites. It boasts a whopping 150 million users and is popular among business owners and individuals alike. The site has managed to achieve quite a lot considering that it only emerged in 2010.

Pinterest used to be huge with foodies and brides-to-be. Today, however, it is a lot more than just a database for recipes and wedding photos. There are numerous images on the website including 75 billion ideas that aptly represent all types of content and users. These users range from millennials to music experts, college professors, students, career civil servants, and even servicemen and women.

Most people used to visit Pinterest to get ideas about various issues and matters. Today however users are visiting the site to shop and view images. And they do really shop on this website. According to a recent study, more than 87% of pinners on the website have purchased something they saw on the website and a whopping 93% plan to do so in the near future.

Demographics

The majority of users on Pinterest are female even though an increasing number of men are beginning to show interest in this site. This is according to a Pew Research study conducted in 2016 of online US-based adults. The study revealed that about 45% of women use Pinterest compared to only 17% of men.

Some of the most popular goods and niches that are of great interest to women on the platform include clothing, home décor, and food. Women also use Pinterest for other purposes such as finding ideas they can use and planning for their futures. Forty-seven percent of users on the website were likely planning for a life event such as a wedding or buying a home or even a trip.

Pinterest is popular with followers of all ages. We have millennials, baby boomers and Generation X all well represented. However, millennials constitute the largest demographic at 36% of all Pinterest users. These are users between the ages of 18 to 29. Baby boomers or people aged between 50 to 65 years constitute 18% of all users on the platform. Therefore, as a business owner or marketer, if you want to target millennials, then Pinterest is a social website that you should consider. There is a good reason for this. Basically, 47% of all millennials on the site have purchased something compared to online 9% on Facebook and 14% on Twitter.

Millennials really do rely on Pinterest to get ideas on what to buy. For instance, over 80% of all millennials on the site while 72% use the pin-board provided on the network to connect with preferred brands. Another 71% logon to the website to find products they need to purchase. This goes to show how crucial this website is to millennials and what a valuable demographic they are for marketers.

Finding your Audience on Social Media

Now that you have a better understanding of the various social media and where your potential customers are, the next step is to actually find out where they really are. When it comes to finding your target audience on the various social networking sites, you need to have a suitable strategy.

First, you need to think about who you need to contact and engage with. To do this successfully, you will need to think beyond the obvious. Think, for instance, who would be interested in your service or products? Take some time and think about these people. Where are they likely to hang out? What age ranges are they? Which social media platforms do they prefer and are they tech-savvy? You need to ask yourself these and numerous other questions. As soon as the answers begin to stream in, you need to take notes and segment these people. They will eventually constitute your customer base across various social media platforms.

Finding people on Twitter

It is easy to search for people on Twitter. The URL www.search.twitter.com is a great place to begin your Twitter search. Use this tool to search for your followers including their locations and demographics. It can help you identify the influencers in your niche and then browse their followers.

You can also use "Twitterrel" to identify and track down users discussing topics related to your industry. You should also make use of relevant hashtags used for particular events or occasions. It is possible to come across excellent people on various hashtags.

Finding people on LinkedIn

LinkedIn is even easier to use. All that you need to do is search for an individual by their name. There is a search box available that you can use to conduct your search. The same search box can be used to search for relevant keywords that will help you find exactly what you are looking for.

During your searches try and use "and" plus "or" if you wish to use multiple keywords. This way, you will be able to search a number of words or each term individually across profiles. It is also possible to search for users using their email addresses. A good idea would be to join a relevant group such as one that is affiliated with your industry or niche.

Finding people on Facebook

You can use Facebook to find people using your email address. Therefore, if you already have an email address of followers, potential leads, and customers, then you can easily find them on Facebook. You can also search for fan pages on Facebook that are relevant to your industry and niche then check out the fans there.

Try and find some key influencers and then check out who their followers are. Connect with more and more people this way because these are your possible customers. Remember to use filters when using the search engines so that you narrow down your search to the kind of followers you want.

Remember that finding followers or customers is a process and not an event. It is something you will keep doing for a while until you have a reasonable following. Therefore, keep searching and keep adding more and more friends and do this consistently for a while.

Tips and advice for business owners and marketers

Always place more focus on social media websites that closely represent your main target audience. There are no distinct social media platforms that completely represent a certain demographic but there us an overlap. You will probably have to select three of four platforms to start with before adding on some more. Having a presence in most of them is crucial, but you do not have to be on all popular social media. Therefore, learn how to prioritize on the best social media to be on.

Focus on audiences on the various platforms and then proceed to target them with suitable or appropriate marketing initiatives. You need to keep in mind that each platform is different therefore ensure that your approach is tailored to each social media's strengths and the kind of audience you are targeting.

Ensure that you create messages that appeal to your audiences, so they feel compelled to listen to you and follow you.

Make use of analytics

Analytics are extremely important because they will provide you with information that you can use. You will receive crucial data as well as an understanding about what is working, who your most loyal followers are, what your customers' demographics are and so much more. This information will enable you to adjust your approach and use methods and processes that actually work and produce results.

You also need to really ignore the larger audience on your preferred platforms. Instead, focus a lot more on your chosen niche and industry and try to capitalize on this specific audience. Remember that social media marketing is pretty competitive because almost all other businesses are also here. Even then, you should mostly focus on your audience and ensure that your efforts are targeted at them. As a brand, you need to always strive for targeted and focused initiatives in order to acquire the results that you desire.

Chapter 3: Customer and Competition Research

As a business owner, you know that you should research your customers as well as your competition. This is because the insights from your research will greatly enhance your marketing strategy and enable you to reach out to even more followers and customers.

However, most people are unaware of how exactly to conduct this research. As a small business or even a startup, you really should learn how to research your potential customers. You should also find out where you need to begin and the kind of useful details you should add to your potential customers.

How well do you know your customer?

It is important that you get to know your customers very well. For instance, you need to find out who they are, what their education levels are, their annual incomes, and the problems that they want to be solved. It is crucial that you also understand some basic details such as how they like their coffee.

There are many reasons why you need to know your customer and understand more about him. According to a recent survey, about 34% of consumers said they broke up with a brand simply because of an irrelevant, disruptive, or poor message. This is a clear indication that companies probably do not understand their customers and do not even bother to research about them.

You need to keep in mind that knowing your customer is more than just guesswork. The ideal situation is to put yourself in their shoes. Find out what their problems, issues, questions, and challenges are. To really understand them, you need to conduct some serious research on your customers. Some of the most effective approaches include one-on-one conversations. These could be via the phone, over a cup of coffee and perhaps even on Skype.

Get on Google Forums

One of the most reliable platforms to learn more about your customers is Google Forum. Google allows people to open groups and then discuss their own personal matters and affairs on them. Business owners can start groups, and their followers or customers can join and leave comments or join discussions.

There are numerous groups as well as discussion forums available. As a business owner, you can log onto these platforms and see what consumers are saying about your industry. It is crucial to spend a bit of time on these forums. Apparently, not many people do this, so you stand a great chance of obtaining useful information. This information can then be used to come up with a better marketing strategy as well as improved products and better services. Find customers within your range and then read the forums and learn about what they are saying. Many will express their problems and challenges. Others will speak about possible solutions. Listen to all these opinions, try and understand where they are coming from, and join in with possible solutions. If they think that you are adding value to their lives by providing solutions, then you will even be able to gain a few more followers and possible customers.

Find blogs related to your niche

You should also search for blogs related to your industry or your niche. Such blogs are often written by industry insiders or experts. They are not just a wealth of information but also a magnet for consumers and others interested in the niche. If you come across blogs with hundreds of comments, take your time to read some of the most prominent comments. These are the ones with the highest number of responses or activity such as likes. Note the author of the comment and see if you can get them to follow you on social media.

Also, try and join in the conversation. Present yourself as an industry insider who has solutions to the problems of the readers. Even as you provide detailed solutions for free, you should find ways of redirecting the consumers to your website. Do this by adding a link to your answer directing readers to your site for further information.

The information that you gather at such a forum is crucial and will provide crucial insights which you can use to better your marketing strategies and improve your customer service and products. Take time to analyze the comments and understand the problems and issues that your potential customers need addressed.

Mix your Sources and Research Methods

At the end of your research and survey, you want to ensure the entire process consists of a balanced quantitative and qualitative research by making use of both secondary and primary sources of information. You need to ensure that when you research a subject, your goal is not simply to get a grip on the statistical group profile but to also appreciate the not-so-obvious nuances of an individual customer as well as their thought process.

There are a couple of simple steps that can get you started with the research process. These will help you to get you started. You can do your research offline and also online. There are various methods available to assist you with both approaches. Below are a couple of easy but effective methods of learning more about your prospects. Some methods require some financial resources while others do not.

Use Talk Walker Alerts, Mention, and Google Alerts

As a business owner or marketer, you need to leverage plenty of information that is available online. This is one way of accessing information about your customers and prospective buyers. One way of doing this is through the site www.google.com/alerts. You can use this site to create an alert for each customer behavior or company then select notification frequency that you prefer. The frequency could be once a day, a couple of times each day, once every two days and so on.

However, Google is not the only website providing this service. There are others who are perhaps even more reliable. There is Mention at www.en.mention.com, and there is Talk Walker Alerts at the URL address www.talkwater.com/alerts. These two websites do a whole lot more compared to Google Alerts as they monitor obscure blogs and social networking websites.

Once you select your preferred site, make sure that you preview the results. This will ensure that you have your parameters correctly set. Should you be trying to monitor a business or a public company, then you will quickly find out about their activities, interests, and initiatives. If you are monitoring the activities of technology consumers, then an instant alert will inform should any relevant news get published.

Also, if you are trying to sell your products and promote your brand, then you will be able to easily monitor useful trends as well as specific prospects and actual customers. These trends will provide you with so much useful information and data that will help you achieve your marketing aims.

Conduct interviews with some of your current customers

An interview with your current customers may seem a little too obvious, but most business owners hardly spend much time talking to their buyers. Your customers are the perfect resource that you need because they have bought products from you or paid for your services and are also easily accessible to you.

Therefore, take the time to speak with your customers and hold interviews with them where possible. Through the interviews, you will get insights into their decision-making process. You will also gain useful content that you will need for any case studies. If you and your customer agree to jointly prepare and promote a case study, then you will both emerge victorious.

You can also conduct a survey in addition to customer interviews. You also have the option of holding or conducting focus group discussions with prospective customers. The main purpose here is to find out what these prospects have in common, what their main sources of information are and also what are some of the challenges they encounter. However, you need to keep in mind that each customer is unique especially for professional services firms. It is sometimes tempting to project the views of one business onto another. This can very likely lead you astray. It is advisable to learn about how to minimize the risk of misusing customer demographics.

Closely study your web analytics

Your web analytics provide you with tons of data which you can use to gain information about your customers. However, you need to first ask yourself some pertinent questions if you are to successfully use this data. For instance, you can ask yourself the following questions;

- What keywords did your customers use to find you?
- What are your visitors' patterns of behavior?
- Where are the visitors from?
- What part of your website did they visit?
- How long do they stay on each page?
- What content format is considered most important?
- Are you able to understand where your customers are along the purchase process?

This information can be utilized to improve your landing pages and website in order to attract more prospects that are interested in your brand and products. This information is also useful if you are considering adopting an inbound marketing system.

Check out your competitors

Another method of acquiring useful information and insights into your potential customers is to check out your competitors. What you need to do is to study the case studies or research published by your competitors. When you review your competitors' case studies, you will get better insights into your prospective customers and the reasons why they chose your competitor instead of your business. Also, apart from just following your competition, you should also follow industry reports and analyst blogs.

Leverage professional social networks

There are large professional networking websites such as Quora and LinkedIn. There are probably plenty of other industry-specific or niche-specific networking websites out there. Try and search for those that are relevant to your niche.

These networks are excellent as they provide you with a huge opportunity for engaging and listening t professionals. You will be able to better understand the frequent challenges and successes of your potential customers. Through these networks, you can ask questions and inquire about additional problems and any solutions they think might be suitable.

You will get an opportunity to ask questions among community members and acquire truly thoughtful and real responses. You will be able to enhance your data that is already in your possession and see how it connects with other people that you know or those who own their own businesses.

Researching your Customers

If you are to successfully know your customers and understand them, then you need to research them. One of the most effective ways of doing this is through personal interviews. This could be one-on-one sessions, discussions over the phone and sometimes on Skype. Such discussions offer some of the most effective ways of getting into your customer's head.

The main challenge is that this method is not scalable should you wish to collect data from a large group of consumers. It is also time-consuming and hence the need for an online solution. Online research can assist with the information gathering process to ensure that you receive the kind of feedback from customers in order to improve your business practices and create better products for them.

Whenever you get online, you need to listen to your customers and generally members within your industry or niche. Therefore, identify the relevant platforms or websites where your customers are likely to be. Some of them include Quora at www.quora.com.

1. Quora

One of the best websites to conduct your research is Quora. This is because this site is full of individuals holding serious conversations and discussions about topical issues and generally a broad range of topics. These can range from immigration to politics to food and so on. All you need to do in order to get started is to enter a keyword into the search query box. The system will serve a list of different conversations featuring your preferred keywords. You can expect one or more of these conversations to reveal what your customers are thinking and how this affects your business.

2. Blog comments

There are different ways of researching using blog comments. For a business owner with a successful blog full of reader comments across different blog posts, you will gain insightful data or information about your market's main problems, issues, and concerns.

There are blogs on the internet that receive hundreds of comments each year. Blog owners often encourage their readers to leave comments and share their thoughts. Such comments provide the blog writer or owner with a wealth of information about what the readers are thinking.

If you do not have your own blog, then consider checking out other blogs within the industry. It is possible to find information pertaining to your niche across various blogs. Therefore, check out different blogs and search for common threads. You can find a particular topic, search across different industry blogs and see what consumers are saying. These comments provide a wealth of information that you can use.

3. Surveys

Another great option that you can use to gather information and thoughts about your customers is the use of surveys. There are long-form surveys often used by businesses to gather information. Surveys are excellent for online customer research. You first need to create a survey and then load it onto one of the popular survey platforms such as Survey Monkey, www.surveymonkey.com. As soon as the survey is ready, all you need to do is send a link to your contacts. You probably have a list of email addresses from your customers. Make use of this mailing list to send out the survey.

If you want the survey to have a high uptake, make sure you offer an incentive. This could be something simple but worthwhile such as a Starbucks gift card or even the chance to win a prize. Sometimes companies even offer to pay individuals who complete surveys. Survey companies like Survey Monkey and others offer to find people that fit your preferred demographics.

Yet another approach that you can use is the short pop-up survey that appears suddenly right at the bottom of a user's website. There are application programs that can help with this such as "Qualaroo" at www.qualaroo.com. You can use this particular approach to confirm a common belief or to test product ideas for your target market. Remember to keep these short surveys as brief as possible. If you can stick to just one question, then you will be alright.

Social media research

One of the most effective ways of researching your customers is through the various social media. It is a fact that social media is a trove of free data about your customers that you can use. If you have access to the right kind of tools, then you can find out a lot about your customers. For instance, you will learn about what questions they are asking and what kind of content they are sharing.

Once you understand this kind of information, you will be able to understand what kind of problems they are facing which will enable you to come up with a solution to their problems. You will also be in a position to define your content and your social media strategies. As a business owner, it is crucial that you learn how to quickly conduct social media research and put the outcome into practice.

Get onto different social networking sites

Your customers are on some of the most popular social media sites including Facebook, Instagram, Twitter, YouTube, and all the others. You will most likely find pages related to your industry on these social platforms. Join these pages and also follow industry leaders. Check out the main posts and the major commentators and influence leaders.

Find out the questions that your customers are asking

Your customers probably have certain challenges, questions, and problems that they are faced with. They often express these questions and challenges on different social media, sharing with others undergoing similar predicaments. If you can join the conversations and provide a solution, you will be able to acquire new customers and address their questions even as you support existing ones. And while at it you should also outline your content strategy which addresses their questions and challenges.

The best solutions that you provide are those that generally address their problems. This means providing practical and useful solutions that actually address the problems that your audience has. You should ensure that your business is structured or modeled to provide solutions to your customers.

You need to note that the best products solve problems and address customers' issues. As such, if you are able to solve a problem with the solutions that you provide, then your customers are more likely to trust you as an expert and buy your products. You can use the following tools to help you with your research.

- Twitter Search
- LinkedIn Answers
- Twitter
- Pinterest
- Facebook Search

Research your competition

Regardless of your industry or niche, you will always have competition. Remember that there are other businesses selling the same products and probably to the same customer base as you. It is possible to check out social media websites in order to find your competition.

Social media users are generally free to choose their preferred social media platforms. They are also free to follow anyone and choose their preferred content to read or consume. Therefore, if you want to attract users to your page, then you have to create content that meets the needs and desires of your users. Ideally, you need to find out which content types work best for them and which ones are not suitable at all.

To learn about your customers' or followers' preferred content types, you will need to learn more about your competitors. There are several ways of researching the competition, and one of them is through social media analytics. Basically, most of your competitors are on various social media, so it is advisable to use the different social media tools in order to track them down.

1. Set up a social media campaign

Let us say you own a business that provides delivery services to pet owners. You specialize in delivering pet food. Such a niche definitely has serious competition. If you want to stand out and outperform your competition, then you have to find out what they are doing wrong and improve on it. You can also perform better where they are performing just right.

Setting up the tools that you need in order to find out more about your competition is really fast and easy. These tools will enable you to compare social media strategies so that you learn what your competitor is up to. If you know the competitors, then that will be easy for you but if you don't then you will need to search and find them.

2. Search across different social media websites

We already know which the top social media websites are. These include Facebook, Twitter, YouTube, Instagram, Snapchat, LinkedIn, Quora, and many others. There are search bars on most of these social websites. Use the search bar as well as other tools provided in order to track down your competition.

When you finally track them down, you will need to read their posts and see what their followers and customers are saying. Try and find out what problems the followers are talking about as well as their challenges. You can also try and identify who the influential followers are and what they are saying to their followers.

You can also place an order from your competition and find out more about their products and services. You will learn about the cost of the products, their shipping times, the kind of after-sales services offered and so much more. This will help you come up with your own strategy.

Do this for about 10 of your main competitors. These are probably businesses operating within your niche and selling to customers that you want to sell to. When you finally find information from most of your competitors, you should analyze it and find out what they are doing wrong and where they are excelling. With this information, you should then be able to come up with an excellent strategy. When you combine all the different ideas from your main competitors, you should now be able to come up with the ultimate social media plan for your business.

Chapter 4: Marketing

The Basics of Social Media Marketing

The average person spends about an hour and a half each day on social media. This amounts to 28% of the time we spend on the internet. This is a significant amount of time considering we run our businesses over the internet and do all other things such as read the mail, pay some bills, do internet banking, and catch up with the news.

Social media marketing

Social media marketing is a crucial aspect of our online businesses. If you get it right, then it will be an endlessly profitable process that will bring in the customers and plenty of money. As a business owner, you need to understand the benefits of understanding and investing in social media marketing.

Social media marketing will help you to promote events, announce new products to your audience, create brand awareness, develop a community of followers and customers, drive leads and sales as well as increase website traffic. This process generally relies on transparency and authenticity.

Getting started

Once you are ready to get started, there are a couple of steps that you should take. These steps provide an excellent opportunity for you to get started. Here they are in the correct order;

1. Determine the goals you wish to optimize for: There are plenty of things that you may wish to promote via social media. It could be your brand, a new product, promote your business and so on.

2. Identify the platforms that suit your business the best: If you are just starting out, then you should start small to enable you to handle the communities across the different social media. You definitely need to get started with Facebook. The second social media site will depend on your business. If you have tangible products, then consider opening an Instagram page.

3. Create a content schedule: As a business owner on social media, you will need to keep your followers and customers engaged. The best approach is to provide your readers with fresh content on a regular basis. In order to get this right, you need to come up with a schedule. You should ideally post between 4 to 7 times each week depending on social media site. On sites such as Twitter, you will have to post almost daily. On others such as Facebook, 3 to 4 times each week is sufficient. Fortunately, there are application programs that can help you to manage this schedule. Think about Agora Pulse at www.agorapulse.com. This website has a content calendar which will post content for you and help with everything else.

4. Source curated content: As a business owner, you are probably busy and may not be able to come up with all the cool content needed for your social media campaigns. Fortunately, you can always search for curated content all across the internet. Share this content with your followers across different platforms.

5. Monitor all your platforms: Always be actively engaged on your social media platforms and observe what kind of relative content within your industry or niche is out there. Also, make sure that you keep engaging your followers and customers. Answer their questions, respond to their comments, and generally get engaged. It is important that you do not ignore your followers or else they may leave.

- *Get fully engaged on social media*

44

There are plenty of businesses just like yours trying to get onto social media. As such, you cannot afford to just have a presence. Instead, you really should actively participate. If you seek to only exist, then you will lose the huge advantage that social media affords businesses.

As an example, about 30% of all millennials on social media engage with a brand at least once each month. Having a presence on different social media will enable you to interact with customers from across the various demographics and help you to gain more customers and increase your profits. Here are some ways of creating a successful social media marketing strategy.

- *Come up with social media market goals*

One of the things that you need to consider as you open social media pages for your brand is to have goals that address some of your biggest challenges. Remember that social media marketing doesn't simply mean checking and checking out. Instead, it should be viewed as a serious event and a major aspect of your overall marketing strategy. Basically, you need to set goals and ensure that all the goals that you set are achievable. If you come up with achievable goals, then you are more likely to be successful in pursuing them.

Also, remember to only have a presence on certain relevant social media in order not to complicate your marketing strategy. You should find only those channels that are suitable for your strategy to avoid over-complicating things. Having a simple approach can take you really far.

Document your social media goals. This is advisable to ensure that you can benchmark and also increase your chances of successfully achieving them. There is strong evidence that suggests those who write down their goals are 30 times more successful compared to those who don't. Some of the goals that you can set to achieve in 2019 may include some of the following;

- Increase your brand awareness
- Improve the quality of sales of your business
- Improve your ROI or return on investment
- Create a loyal fan base
- Keep an eye on the competition

- *Research your social media audience*

It is said that almost 80% of all adults are on Facebook and log in regularly to catch up with friends and generally interact with others. It is crucial that you research and understand your audience. This is necessary so that you find out exactly who your customers are, what their ages are, their income levels, and all other kinds of information.

- *Engage your audience and do NOT ignore them*

Social networking websites are designed for engagements. All the people who use social media do so in order to discuss, share, converse, and generally engage with other users.
As a business owner, you cannot afford to ignore these crucial followers. Your audience is really important. It is from this following that you will get your leads, traffic to your website and even customers. Therefore, answer their questions, respond to their queries, share their content and basically engage with them in any way possible.

Also, remember to post your content at the best times possible. There are times that are ideal for posting on most social sites. Find out what the best times are for your preferred channels and then post your content at these times. You should also ensure that you have a community manager ready to respond to posts and questions from your followers.

- *Keep track of your efforts*

As a business owner, you should keep a close eye on your social media performance. Analyzing your efforts and checking out your metrics is important. You should analyze your efforts and monitor your performance so that you understand what strategies work and what approaches need improvement. It is crucial to generally be on the lookout on the performance of your social media pages at all times.

- *Consistency*

As a business owner, you need to ensure consistency across all your social media pages. For instance, you need to ensure that your "About Us" page and your social media Home Pages have the same cover photos and usernames. This kind of consistency gives you credibility and tells your followers that you can be trusted. It is also easy to recognize your pages from one social media site to another.

If you are on Instagram, then you should ensure that you have a daily story. Instagram users appreciate fresh content provided on a regular basis. Make sure that you share this story on your Facebook page as well. This should be easy as these two sites are interconnected.

- *Listed*

You should get listed on all your social media pages so that your customers can search for you and actually find you. It is important that your followers, customers, and all others are able to find you when they search for you. If they cannot find your page, then they most likely will find someone else.

- *Provide useful content*

As a business owner with followers across different social media platforms, you should take time to develop useful content that adds value to your followers or audience.

Your audience and followers have certain problems and issues which are common within your industry. As a business owner, you need to research what these problems are and then find solutions. Provide content and answer these questions the best way that you can.

Your aim here is to answer the questions that your viewers have. Do this regularly across different platforms. Let them eventually get to trust you as an authority on those specific issues. If they begin to trust you, then you can redirect them to your blogs and websites. From here on you can groom your followers into paying customers. The principle here is very simple. First, give, give, and then give some more before you eventually start receiving. This principle works perfectly all the time.

Use apps to post your content

48

As a business owner, you are probably busy attending to your customers and business most of the day. You probably lack the time to develop and post content on social media on a regular basis. Just the knowledge that you have to develop content for each of your social media accounts can be daunting.

The good news is that you do not have to break your back developing fresh content every day. There are plenty of apps that can help with this. One of them is Muse Cam. This is an application that helps you to shoot great images on the iOS platform. The images can then be edited using advanced tools and other features.

You can also use an app known as Boomerang. This is an application that takes a series of great images in quick succession. The effect is to create a GIF-like image that you can then share on your various social media platforms. There are plenty of other tools that can actually schedule your social media content posting for an entire week or so. This saves you the time and effort of having to log onto each of your social media platforms in order to post and share content.

Guerilla Marketing

The term guerrilla marketing may conjure up images of rebellion and conflict. However, when it comes to marketing, this is not the case. When this concept is applied to marketing, it takes on a different meaning.

Guerilla marketing is a type of marketing and advertising strategy that focuses on low-cost strategies that provide maximum yields. Many marketers view guerilla marketing as an extremely unconventional form of marketing which, however, is very effective. Due to its unconventional nature, guerrilla marketing is not easy to explain but is best understood when observed.

Alternative advertising

Guerilla marketing is a form of alternative advertising. It differs from mainstream advertising and is preferred because of its relatively low cost as well as effectiveness in getting the message out.

The aim of this form of marketing is to take the customer by complete surprise. The advertising messages have a much more powerful impact on consumers compared to traditional ads. This is largely because guerrilla ads aim to affect the consumer at a more memorable and personal level.

Guerilla marketing tactics

Guerrilla marketing adverts are much more suitable for small businesses seeking to advertise to a large base of consumers but without the budget to do so. Sometimes large corporations also use this marketing approach, especially when conducting grassroots campaigns. However, they do so to complement their other marketing campaigns. Individuals have also adapted guerrilla marketing tactics. They use this approach when they seek to find more work or to get noticed in a crowd.

Large businesses

While this particular marketing tactic is ideal for small businesses with limited budgets, many large corporations are adopting it. Their budgets are already large, and brands established. Even then, they prefer guerrilla marketing tactics to enhance their overall marketing strategy.

However, such approaches are risky when adapted by big businesses. In some cases, these tactics have been known to collapse, and flop miserably. When this happens, it becomes a total PR nightmare for the companies involved, and they have to readjust their strategies. Fortunately, small businesses stand no such risks and are able to engage in guerrilla marketing successfully.

Guerilla marketing, and small businesses

If you own a small business, then guerilla marketing may be the ideal marketing strategy. The reason is that, if you have a good ad, and execute it well, then the effect will be far reaching while the cost will be relatively low. Guerrilla ads provide an excellent way of getting noticed and help to distinguish you from the competition.

Budget-friendly ads

Guerrilla marketing is a favorite with small business owners because it is an affordable approach to advertising. What is essential is actually coming up with a catchy, creative ad that is well thought-out, and well presented. The ad implementation does not have to be costly, but creativity is also necessary here. Guerilla marketing is seen as a type of time investment rather than financial.

Types of guerilla marketing

There are different types of guerrilla marketing. While these are very few, it is good to learn about them, and see how they apply in real life situations. Yes this is a Social Media Marketing Guide however this does not mean you ignore other way of gaining extra traffic to stay ahead of everyone else!

1. Outdoor guerrilla marketing: This type of approach makes use of existing street furniture or anything out on the street. For instance, a marketer can place a temporary advertising message onto a statue, a park bench, street light, and so on. Even artworks will do. These can be strategically placed on sidewalks or walls across streets.

2. Indoor guerrilla marketing: This type of guerrilla advertising is very similar to the indoor guerrilla marketing. The only difference is that this type takes place outdoors in places such as a railway station, university campuses, and shops. It is just as effective as the ads are personal and targeted at individuals.

3. Event ambush guerilla marketing: People do attend events, and sometimes in great numbers. If you have a relevant product or provide a related service, then you can leverage this audience especially in the process of the event. It could be a sporting event or a convert or any other. This doesn't really matter. However, take the opportunity presented by the event to market, and promote your product. Do this in a noticeable way and without necessarily seeking permission from the program organizers or sponsors.

4. Experiential guerrilla marketing: This approach includes all of the above examples. The only difference is that it calls for interactions with viewers or audience. Audience members will, in this case, be expected to interact with the brand for maximum effect.

Approaches to creating guerrilla ads

First, identify the most pressing problem that your products or service solves. Now be creative and think about the kinds of unconventional solutions to solve the problem. Broadcast this message unconventionally, and possibly without using words.

Consider things that your audience members regularly pass by each day but without giving them much thought. Take these things, and use them to do something out of the ordinary.

Guerrilla marketing has now gone digital. Therefore, think about all the places that your target audience is especially online. They could be on various social media sites such as Facebook, Twitter, Instagram, and other sites. Think about creative ambush ads and give them a show they will always remember. While you shouldn't encourage lying, you should be creative and come up with eye-popping and possibly even shocking but positive guerrilla marketing ads.

Chapter 5: Popular Social Media Marketing Sites

As a business owner seeking to grow your business, attract more customers, promote your brand and generally be profitable, you will need to come up with an appropriate marketing strategy that will work for your business. One of the most effective ways of doing this is to go multichannel. This means using different channels to promote the business, market the products, and advertise the brand.

Social media marketing has become the most crucial platform for all businesses both large and small. Digital marketing has focused a lot more on social media and it is a trend that no business owner can afford to miss out on. Social media marketing is about building unique relationships and engaging with online users because they have the potential of becoming your customers one day.

Why choose social media marketing?

A lot of business owners still do not understand why they need to use social media. They still haven't understood the reach and power of these social networking websites. A lot of them still think that social media sites are a waste of time where users gossip and spend time doing non-productive activities. Some business owners even prohibit their employees or workers from accessing social networking sites at work.

The failure of all these people to understand and fathom the power of social media is causing them to lose out on the numerous advantages that these platforms have to offer. They should copy and follow what numerous other business owners are doing. A lot of enterprising individuals and firm owners have come to understand and appreciate the power of social media.

Two basic ways of using social media

There are two main methods of using social networking sites as part of your marketing strategy. These include word-of-mouth, advice and all recommendations from friends and family. This kind of confidence will boost your business and promote your brand. This particular piece of advice holds true both online and offline. Social media sites have now become the online equivalent of traditional word-of-mouth marketing technique.

With social media, you are able to read, comment, share and generally interact with others when a message is posted. This is a powerful way of getting a message out to consumers. Business owners are able to make use of social media to implement their digital marketing campaigns. All that they need to do is to create the relevant content and then share it on social media. Others will pick it up from there.

However, the content will need to add value to the lives of social media users. They need to see some value in the content that you post as a business owner. Therefore, take your time to think about appropriate content that your viewers would love to see. To do this effectively, you will have to understand them and know what their main problems, issues, and challenges are. Once you have an understanding of their issues and challenges, you will be able to create quality content that is interesting to read or watch, fun, and adds value.

There is another way of using social networking websites for marketing a small business online. This is through the use of paid advertising. A lot of all the major social media sites provide ways for businesses to advertise their merchandise. The advertising can attract a huge following and with far-reaching effects at very affordable rates. Many users of social networks receive advertising messages every once in a while. A lot of them follow the messages if they are well presented.

As a business owner, you need to understand and learn how to combine these two techniques in order to promote your business, enhance your brand, and increase your sales. These two strategies, when combined properly, can propel your business to great heights and provide you with the kind of success that you could only dream about.

Advantages of Social Media Advertising

There are numerous advantages of advertising on social media. One of these benefits is direct interaction with customers. It is not easy for businesses to get into contact with customers. This would normally cost a lot of money and small businesses do not have this kind of money.

However, through social media websites, business owners can reach an extremely large base of potential customers as well as general social media users and followers. Interacting with customers gives you a chance to learn about their wants and needs, what works and what doesn't as well as generally learn about who they are and where they live.

You are able to reach out to a broader or wider audience than what is possible through traditional marketing methods. Social media sites such as Facebook, Twitter, and Instagram have followers in the billions or hundreds of millions in most cases. Gaining access to such a large pool of users propels you to an advantageous position.

You also get to reach out to a targeted audience. While it is common to advertise to a wide audience using traditional marketing methods, social media allows you to market your business and brand to a smaller and more localized audience. This targeted audience is probably one that has a direct interest in your products and the services that you provide.

Instagram for Business

Create an appealing and creative Instagram profile

Instagram is a globally popular social networking website. It is well known as the best site for sharing photos, videos, and images of all kinds. If you have a tangible product that you are selling, then beautiful photos that are large, clear, and colorful will fair very well on this platform. Business owners need to have an Instagram page which can be used to interact with members and share images and videos in order to promote their brands and businesses.

Instagram has over 800 million users each day who spend roughly thirty minutes browsing through images and videos on the platform. Such a huge daily audience presents plenty of opportunity for your business and brand. However, you first need to create an appealing business page.

To do this, you will need to be very creative. Remember there are plenty of other businesses within your niche. As such, you need to bring you're A-game to the table. This means creating a professional website that contains your business name and clearly displays your brand name.

Include your business address, official name, online address such as your URL, and ensure that you are consistent with the images, brand, and business name. Instagram allows you to provide sufficient contact and business information.

You should follow this by providing absolutely clear and beautiful images that are captivating and memorable. Tell a story with each image and allow your audience to enjoy the images, share your posts and interact in any other way.

Increase your Instagram reach using these simple tricks

There are many reasons why Instagram account holders need a large following. If you want to increase your reach, then you will need to increase the visibility of your posts. Reach simply refers to the people who get to view your posts. When more people get to view your posts, you will get more followers and hopefully more customers. Here are some tips on how to skyrocket your reach.

1. Ensure that you place your posts at the right time: The most important step in increasing your reach is having the right kind of post. Once you have the right, you should post it at the correct time. Timing is important because you want your audience to view the post. Find out when they are most active and available to check out their Instagram.

2. Have your primary goal as engagements: If you want to increase your reach on Instagram, then you need to focus more on engagement. This should be your number one focus. First, create relevant and engaging content for your viewers. The content could be contests or giveaways. You could also ask some questions and basically engage your readers and followers. And remember to always include a call to action. For instance, you could say, "Tag a friend," "Follow this link," and so on.

And remember to keep the engagements in motion. Respond to queries, answer questions from your followers, share any content they share with you and generally engage them. Never ignore them otherwise you will not be able to hang on them for long.

3. Your hashtags should be optimized: Hashtags are important on major social media platforms such as Instagram. You need to make sure that you choose the right hashtags and then optimize them appropriately. Suitable hashtags are those that are related to your specific niche or industry. Posts with 11 or more hashtags tend to attract the highest engagements even though Instagram allows up to 30 hashtags per post. Always think about the marketing terms relevant to your niche. These are terms that your audience is probably searching for on social media. Use these terms on your posts and hashtags for a much wider reach.

4. Make use of video content: Video content on Instagram is said to attract a lot more attention compared to other content types. Users will engage much more on video than other posts. They are capable of generating double the engagements on other posts. You want your posts to attract more viewers and hence comments and likes will help to attract a lot more people to your page.

5. Promote user-generated content: You should recognize and acknowledge your followers. Sometimes you will find content from your followers. This content could be photos or videos for instance. First, curate this content and just focus on the most crucial parts. Once the content is ready, make sure to share it with your followers. An analysis of Instagram has shown that user-generated content greatly increases conversion rate. This rate increases, even more, when users interact with the shared post.

The Lifestyle / Business Model

There are generally two paths to follow when starting or running your own business. You could come up with a startup business or a lifestyle business. Startups are generally very involving and require huge amounts of capital. On the other hand, a lifestyle business is one where the owner is often the sole employee of the business and earns sufficient amounts to take care of his needs as well as the freedom to pretty much do whatever he or she wants.

A lot of startups fail. Generally, for every successful business such as Instagram, there are hundreds of others out there that failed miserably or barely surviving. You cannot afford to start a business whose chances of success are only 50% or less. This is why a lifestyle business model is more suitable for you compared to a startup.

Startups take up a lot of your time. You generally have to work from nine to five. While this can be exciting for a while, it can become exhausting. On the other hand, a lifestyle business allows you to work whenever you want and from any location around the world just as long as you have access to the internet.

Tools, apps, and software to increase your reach

If you want to increase your reach on Instagram, then you should do so using a number of tools and apps. There are more than 30 different tools, apps, and software that you can use to increase your reach. If you seriously want to enjoy huge growth and long-term success, then you should promote your brand and increase its visibility. Here are some tools and apps to help you along.

1. Viral Upgrade: This is basically a growth platform used by both influencers and brands. If you use this platform, you will be assigned an assistant who will help you to grow your account. The assistant will grow your account organically by engaging with your audience and growing your base. You will provide the desired demographics and the assistants will help with this.

2. Hoot Suite: It is important to post content regularly on your Instagram page. However, you are probably busy and cannot maintain a regular posting schedule. Fortunately, Hoot Suite can do exactly that for you. This is software designed to help with your scheduling. It will find suitable and appropriate content for your niche, caption the posts, and post on schedule.

3. Sprout Social: Success on social media platforms like Instagram is often gauged based on engagement. This means the number of likes, followers, comments and so on. This app enables you to view your engagements with followers as well as access to more useful data. For instance, you can find out the time when the most people view your posts and so on. You can also pre-schedule content posting and make the entire process faster, easier, and more organized.

4. Repost: Yet another useful software tool that you can use to increase your Instagram reach is Repost. This tool allows you to post images that you do not have a right to. It then gives credit to the poster. This way, you are able to post content or images from all over the web without flouting any copyright rules.

5. Social Insight: Sometimes it is difficult for brands to interact with each other and with followers due to time and size of followers. Fortunately, Social Insight allows businesses to manage and organize followers as well as scheduling posts at particular times. You can also receive analytics, so you learn what works and what does not.

Facebook

Facebook is the world's largest social networking website with more than 2 billion active users each month. As a small business owner and manager, you should have a presence on Facebook. This way, you will be able to use the opportunities available to reach out to this massive population. There are numerous marketing opportunities, brand promotion, and others that you can enjoy. You can have a Facebook business page, location page, or even be part of a group. Once you have a presence on Facebook and the page is live, you can then begin taking advantage of all the opportunities available.

Facebook groups

A Facebook group is a must-have for all local businesses. They are also essential for all other small businesses including those based online. Facebook recently made it possible for page owners to open groups relating to their own unique niches and feeds.

There are over 1 billion individuals that use Groups on Facebook. It is within the groups that like-minded users actually connect. This is why opening a group is important. Once you open a group page within Facebook, then you will attract hundreds of interested persons who are easier to engage with because of shared interests.

Facebook groups also provide analytics which will provide you with insights on how your group is performing and which tactics are working. Facebook groups come with group chats, built-in analytics, create polls and post documents, and notifications to members.

Skyrocketing your Facebook reach

There are certain things that you can do in order to enhance and increase your Facebook reach. It is your reach that will enable you to get more followers and expose your brand even further. Here are some ways you can do this.

1. Optimize content and then share it on Facebook

One of the things that you need to do on your Facebook page is to share content. When you share content, you engage your followers and possibly also their followers. Make sure that the content you share is outstanding, memorable, and evokes a reaction from viewers. Such content is likely to be shared by your followers. To reach an even wider audience, you should optimize your content. Optimizing means using hashtags and adding what is relative to your niche and industry.

2. Less is more so post less content

You need to try and post less content if you want to impact your viewers. Many times, Facebook users post a lot of content which sometimes overwhelms the audience who consider it spamming. Try and focus on very high-quality images or videos which are shared possibly once a day for a total of 4 days each week.

3. Engage your audience

You should always engage your audience, viewers, and followers. If they share any content, then make sure you engage. You can leave a comment, like, or share with your followers. If you post content and your viewers leave comments, make sure you respond to these comments. You could answer their questions, like their statements, and basically, engage them.

4. Target repeat visitors Facebook ads and emails

To reach out to more viewers and engage them even further, you should use indirect methods such as using ads and emails. Since you already have the right audience, it becomes very easy to reach out and promote your brand and advertise your products. Facebook has made it very easy for small businesses to engage their followers and reach out to a wider audience through groups and business pages.

5. Boost some of your best posts

You also need to focus on boosting some of your best posts. This is yet another way of reaching out to more viewers and increasing your reach. First, you should produce top-notch content. Any content that accumulates numerous engagements such as likes and shares can be promoted so that it reaches even more people across Facebook.

The Lifestyle – Business Model

There are different kinds of lifestyle businesses. However, most people think about a business where the founder pursues a passion and then forms a business around it. Like they say, "follow your passion and build a business around it." IF this approach is properly executed, then your business will thrive for years to come.

If you have a hobby, then you can build a business around it. In this case, instead of a blog, you should open a Facebook page. One of the challenges you can expect with this kind of business is traffic. Fortunately, Facebook has millions of users and account holders many of who share your interest. You stand a great chance of finding interested followers, fans, leads, and customers through Facebook.

This business approach is extremely beneficial compared to other businesses. Since you mostly do what you like, you get to enjoy every minute of it. And you do not have to work on your business on a full-time basis. You can choose your hours depending on when demand is high or when it gets busy.

Passion business is suitable for most people because there is no need for huge capital investments. You do not need a lot of money to get started like you would with other types of businesses such as a brick-and-mortar establishment or a startup.

Another benefit of this business approach is that you can manage it mostly from your social media pages. As a business person, you can take advantage of all the conveniences provided by social networking websites such as Facebook in order to get the word out, reach out to interested people, and get followers and customers.

Selling points of the lifestyle business approach

You get to grow as fast or as slow as you please. There is no pressure, no shareholders, and no urgency at all but only what you want. A lifestyle business is designed to provide you with a comfortable lifestyle. It is up to you to define the comfort you desire.

You do not have to fall sick working for someone else. A lot of people put on weight because they have to sit for long hours working at someone else's business. If you want to head to the gym or prepare a meal in the afternoon, you are at liberty to do so.

You do not have to be tech-savvy to start your own business. You can start your own business and manage it well without having to come up with a technical project. This approach is suitable for all people. However, research has shown that it favors women a lot more especially because of the challenges they experience at the traditional workplace. Think about all the challenges women have and then consider the kind of freedom that this business approach has to offer.

Tools, apps, and software to increase reach and ease things up

There are numerous tools available that you can use on Facebook to enhance your business activities. There are some excellent tools that you can use to help you to come up with custom

Facebook pages and so much more. While most of them are free to use, there is a limitation when it comes to accessible features. Here are some tools that you can use.

1. Heyo: Heyo is a great tool that you can use on your Facebook business account. You can use it to create hashtag campaigns, contests, and sweepstakes. This tool will help to save you time as it provides free Facebook templates. You get creative control with the drag and drop editor. You also get to increase your reach via photo contests, sweepstakes, group deals and so much more.

2. Tab Site: Another interesting app that you can use with your Facebook page is Tab Site. This app enables you to create and then manage your very own custom Facebook pages. You also get to create and manage your Facebook apps and hold promotions. Tab Site also allows you to offer contents, deals, and multiple apps. The apps need no coding or programming and easy to use. You can use them for pixel perfect designs. You also able to do other things such as run video and photo contests, add product slideshows, add YouTube videos, import blog posts, run sweepstakes, and so much more.

3. Short Stack: The software Short Stack is a powerful tool used for app creation. It allows you, the user, to create powerful apps, campaigns, and landing pages without the need to learn anything new. Other things that you can do with this software program include unlimited campaigns, promotions, 5000 campaign visits per 30 days, export entries and leads, and so much more.

4. Woo Box: Woo Box is an app that helps Facebook users to run and manage campaigns on the platform. Numerous businesses use Woo Box for different purposes including the use of six different apps, to customize their Facebook tabs, HTML Fangate, photo contests, and so much more. This is an excellent tool to support all of your Facebook marketing, ad, and promotions.

5. Easy Tab Creator: This software is another that you can use with your Facebook business page. It features a pretty simple interface and can help you to manage up to three different pages absolutely free. This application runs on Facebook and enables you to customize your business page by adding all kinds of content including YouTube videos, text, and so on.

YouTube

YouTube is the second largest search engine and the largest video sharing platform on the internet. Users can share, post, and watch videos on YouTube for free. All you need to do is open an account which is easy if you already have a Gmail account. It is a very popular website with users from across America and all over the world.

Users visit the website to watch interesting, entertaining, and captivating videos, to learn through videos, and to obtain news and information. If you join YouTube, you will be able to post videos and share it with the hundreds of millions of users who log in every day to watch entertaining content. Most people who get onto YouTube do so to for information and entertaining. Take advantage of the 1.6 billion active monthly users to leverage and market your brand and business.

Skyrocket your YouTube traffic reach

1. Only post high-quality videos: If you want to be successful on YouTube and increase your reach, then you should focus on producing only high quality, exciting, memorable, and engaging videos. Make a point of learning how to produce good quality content which you can then share on your YouTube page for wider reach.

2. Make use of tools and apps to increase traffic: There are lots of tools provided by YouTube that you can use to increase your reach. For instance, you can use video editing tools and apps to improve the quality of your videos. This way, more people will view and share your content, increasing your reach.

3. Optimize your content: You are probably used to optimizing content for your blog or website. Now you need to learn to optimize content for YouTube as well. YouTube is a large search engine second only to Google. Therefore, optimize your videos so as to increase your reach.

4. Engage your viewers: All too often we tend to ignore our followers and those who comment on our videos. This is wrong and definitely not good for business. As a business owner seeking to increase your reach, you should engage your viewers, respond to their comments, and definitely encourage them to share the videos.

5. Post videos regularly: You need to post high quality, suitable edited and entertaining videos on a regular basis. Doing so will keep you relevant and will keep your viewers coming back for more. You will also enable them to share more of your content with their networks which is excellent as it increases your reach.

The lifestyle business model for YouTube

If you want to start your own stress-free business, then the best approach is to start a lifestyle business rather than any other. This kind of model allows you to create a business based on your passion.

Other business models such as brick-and-mortar may require you to remain open from 8.00 am to 5.00 pm, demand lots of hard work, and are possibly stressful. However, building a business around a hobby and passion allows you to work only as hard as you like and whenever you want. You can choose to work only mornings or only evenings then go to the gym or park and relax.

Businesses such as startups and others require large capital inputs and you have to search for investors or borrow loans. This will put you under a lot of pressure. Most startups never live beyond the first year, and the rest probably won't see the end of the fifth year.

If you start a lifestyle business, you can put it on social media platforms such as YouTube and find customers here. Your talent and passion will attract numerous like-minded people who will then become your followers and eventually your customers. You can expand exponentially through social media yet expend very little energy. It is advisable to focus on this business model compared to all others.

Tools, apps, and software to ease things and increase reach

Building a YouTube channel takes a lot of work especially if you are trying to grow your business. Fortunately, there are some amazing tools that you can use to help you with your channel. These tools and apps will help you to manage your channel, increase your reach, and edit your videos. Here are some of the tools and apps that you can use to enhance your YouTube channel.

1. Tube Buddy: Tube Buddy is considered the single most useful YouTube toolkit. It is an essential toolkit that you need to have if you are to be successful. It comes with more than 60 different features that help you with almost anything that you need. Tube Buddy will generally help you to promote your channel and videos, ensure that you are productive, and also aid with your YouTube SEO.

2. Snappa: If your YouTube channel is to grow and increase your reach, then you need a tool that lets you create excellent artwork and images. Snappa is among the top tools out there for YouTube videos. It will enhance your videos and enable you to come with great visuals through its premade templates. It is advisable to always use high-quality image editing and enhancing tools for your YouTube and Snappa is excellent even when compared to other tools in the market.

3. Creator Studio App: If you have a number of apps and wish to promote your business through them, then you will need some assistance. This is where the Creator Studio app comes in handy.

This is a powerful tool that lets you do just about everything on your YouTube channel except perhaps creating the original video. You also get to find out how your video is performing and receive metrics and lots of other things as well.

4. Wix: You will need this app if you plan to monetize your YouTube account. As a small business owner, your aim of using social media sites like YouTube is to help you find customers in order to sell your products for a profit. For this to happen successfully, you will need a website. There are plenty of website builders out there, but Wix is absolutely the best of them all. It is super easy to use and lets you design your website using amazing templates. You will not even need to learn coding.

5. Buffer: If you want to increase your reach, you will need to share your videos across different social media platforms. One of the best tools to share your videos is Buffer. This handy tool enables you to share your videos across different social media platforms. It helps you to schedule content posting on various social networks allowing you to save time while still maintaining a credible presence on these networks.

Twitter

As a social media platform, Twitter has grown to become a useful site and all businesses should consider having a presence here. Users get on Twitter to catch up with the latest news, share stores, videos, images, and so much more.
Now since almost all businesses and users are on Twitter, it is easy to get lost unless you make an effort to stand out. This is the only way to stand out on Twitter. Here is how you can skyrocket your reach on Twitter.

1. Get to know your audience: There are hundreds of millions of users who check out Twitter each day. Not all these Twitter users are your audience though. You want your tweets and all other posts to be viewed by the right people who are your target audience. Therefore, find people interested in your niche, those discussing industry matters and those searching for your products. If you are able to identify your audience, then you will get off to a great start.

2. Make use relevant hashtags: If you want to reach more people, especially those relevant to your industry, then you need to use hashtags that relate to your niche. Most people on Twitter use hashtags regularly as they bundle people together. Whenever you produce content, try and include a couple of hashtags. Keep them short and never use more than three at a time.

3. Engage your audience and talk with them: Your audience will comment on your posts, share, ask questions, and generally engage with your brand. As a business owner, you should talk to your audience and followers. Respond to their comments, answer their questions, share their posts and generally make sure that you engage in a positive manner, so they feel worthy and appreciated.

4. Find the best times to tweet and post content: Twitter is among other time-sensitive platforms. You need to know when to post your content. It has been noted that the best time to tweet is 5.00 pm for highest retweets and between 12.00 noon and 6.00 pm to have the highest reach. However, this does not work the same way for all brands. Fortunately, there are apps such as Follower Wonk and Audiense that can help you to figure out the best ad posting times.

5. Post content regularly: Content on Twitter has a very brief lifespan. Something posted in the morning may become obsolete before lunchtime. This is common on Twitter rather than other social networks. Therefore, post content about 4 times per day about 5 days each week. This way, you will help your brand to remain relevant.

How to sell the lifestyle-business model

One of the best ways to start a successful online business is to pursue the lifestyle business model. This model is renowned because it is centered on your hobby and passion. As such, you are not under serious pressure for any reason and can choose when to work and how much to work.

A business that is focused around your passion does not need to cost a lot of money to establish and set up. Most of your work can be done online and only when you want to. For instance, you will not need to spend money or incur expenses finding customers. All your customers can be sourced from social media sites. Twitter is an excellent platform that you can use to establish your business and reach out to potential customers. You will find plenty of customers via social media especially if you use the right hashtags and focus on individuals interested in your niche. The lifestyle business will not stress you out unnecessarily as there is no rent to pay, no loans to service and no bosses to answer to.

Tools and software to ease things for you and increase reach

Twitter is a fantastic platform for business. If you wish to grow your business and find new followers and customers, then you need to be on this platform. However, this might prove to be a challenge because most other businesses in your industry are also here.

Fortunately, with the use of tools, you can make things easier for you. There are tools that help with curating and sharing content, scheduling posting, increasing reach and so much more. Here is a look at some tools that will help you get ahead.

1. Hoot Suite: One of the best and most versatile tools that you need for your Twitter account is Hoot Suite. This tool is fantastic at getting you organized. You can post all your tweets as well as photos and videos via this amazing tool. Hoot Suite can help you schedule posting so that you prepare content which is then posted at a more appropriate time. You also get to keep a track of what is happening on your account.

2. Buffer: Automatic posting is something you need to consider especially if you are a heavy Twitter user. As a business owner, you are probably quite busy and need help with your social media accounts. Buffer is the tool that you need to accomplish this task. It can post content on your behalf across multiple social platforms and allow you to attend to other matters.

3. Twitter Counter: Yet another tool available to Twitter users is Twitter Counter. This tool provides graphs and basic analytics about tweets and followers. You can learn about the statistics and figures for each day, week, and month. The tool also creates content automatically and produces statistics in real time.

4. Social Oomph: This is a tool that provides you with lots of services that you need. Services include auto following anyone who follows you on Twitter. The app allows you to create automated messages which are sent as replies to your followers. It also enables you to schedule future tweets, so you do not have to worry about your social media when you are attending to other duties.

5. Tweet Adder: One of the best tools out there for adding Twitter followers to your account very fast is Twitter Adder. This particular tool easily adds about 150 followers in your niche each day. These are real followers who are within your industry and are genuinely interested in your niche. When followers are added to your account, this tool sends them an automated thank you message and also does replies.

Pinterest

Social media has changed the way we do business. We are now able to create communities and direct traffic to our websites and at the same time develop lasting relationships. One platform that is capable of all these is Pinterest. This platform that is, however, not utilized as much as it should. Yet it can direct plenty of traffic your way and increase your reach.

1. Create Pinterest pins that direct to valuable sites: Pinterest now focuses on displaying pins leading to valuable resources and blog posts. You may have a beautiful image, but if it does not lead to any useful resources, then it will not be prominently displayed. Therefore, come up with a useful website or blog and ensure your pins redirect there.

2. Grow both your reach and followers: While it is important to gain as many followers as possible, you should focus more on creating pins that are likely to reach people not using Pinterest. For instance, think about pins so great that your followers will share with others so that they go viral. This way, you stand a chance of going viral and possibly reaching millions of people.

3. Make use of keywords on board names: Your boards will appear on interest feeds and in the "Picked for You" list if there is a relevant and suitable title. For instance, if you are targeting tourists, then your board can have a title like Travel Tips.

4. A number of keywords should be used: Pinterest mostly resembles a search engine where millions of individuals carry out searches looking for ideas, for gifts, and all manner of things. Your brand and businesses are more likely to be found by these millions of potential customers when you use the correct keywords. Therefore, always think beyond your current followers, use relevant keywords, and reach out even to people, not on Pinterest.

5. Join a Group Board: You need to consider joining board groups in order to increase your reach. Many business owners and individuals join group boards in order to have pins exposed to as many people as possible. Take time to identify relevant group boards. This way, your pins will be exposed to hundreds of thousands of people within the same group.

The lifestyle-business model

There are numerous different business ideas that you can choose. However, some require a lot of capital while others demand a lot of your time and attention. If you do not have a lot of time or attention, then you probably want to start a lifestyle business. A lifestyle business is generally created out of a hobby or passion that you have. Such a business is highly likely to be successful because you probably understand everything about it, have passion and enjoy doing things related to it. You do not need a lot of resources to get started. You are free to start small and grow at your own pace.

Therefore, you do not need to borrow money from family and friends to get started. You also do not need to seek investor funding as most startups do. Many startups fail within the first year and most others will not get to their third birthday. However, most lifestyle businesses succeed because of the simplicity of the business as well as the passion of the business owner and freedoms that it has to offer.

Remember that a successful business is one that affords you freedom, one where you determine the pace, and one where you have a healthy balance between work and relaxation only a lifestyle business can afford you this kind of success even in the long term.

Tools and apps to increase reach and ease things for you

Pinterest is fast becoming among the most trusted and best apps that people use when they need information. Putting your business on this platform is a major plus. However, you need to work a little harder if you want to beat the competition and succeed. If you are managing multiple channels, then you will need some help with your social media accounts. Fortunately, that help is readily available through tools, software, and apps. Here are some tools that can help you achieve success on Pinterest.

1. Buffer: Buffer is a tool that helps you find great pins from different websites which are then added instantly to your Pinterest account. Also, you could be browsing across Pinterest and notice something that catches your eye. You could easily pin this to your social media accounts using a tool provided on Buffer. Another useful feature is that you have access to stats showing how your pins are performing. These include likes, re-pins, and comments.

2. Tailwind: This is a great tool for your Pinterest account and can help you manage almost all activities. It also comes with some interesting analytics, so you get the statistical information that you need. Therefore, you are able to schedule posts, receive important statistics and also get to analyze the competition and see the activity of your influential followers.

3. ViralWoot: ViralWoot is a useful Pinterest tool that offers a number of exciting features. These include a tool for growing your followers, one for scheduling, another for pin alerts, and one for placing advertisements. However, it is not free and there is a monthly fee to pay.

4. Loop88: This is a tool designed to specifically help you to increase reach and gain more followers. Loop88 is a Pinterest tool that connects your account to important influencers within your industry. The influencers, especially those with engaged followers are connected with brands and advertisers. You will enjoy lots of re-pins, exposure, and numerous additional followers.

5. Pinterest widgets: This consists of a free list of tools that you can use in order to integrate your website with your Pinterest account. There are about five separate widgets. The first is the pin it button which enables you to pin images from your website. Then there is the follow button which makes it easy for people to follow you on Pinterest directly from your website. Others are the profile, board, and pin widgets all of which play a crucial role in integrating your site and Pinterest account.

LinkedIn

The social website LinkedIn is thought of as the Facebook or social media for business. A lot of business executives and professionals do not see much need for platforms such as Facebook and Instagram find a welcoming home on LinkedIn. This is because LinkedIn connects them with businesses, business leaders, other professionals, and work-related opportunities. If you have a LinkedIn account, there are ways that you can increase your reach and promote your presence. Here are some of these ways

Skyrocket your reach on LinkedIn

1. Start by optimizing your page: LinkedIn generally wants its members to have complete profiles so that it's easy for others to track them down and recognize them. It also makes it easy to access opportunities and connect with others. For instance, you should provide all your official names, an address, and contact information. Also, make use of relevant keywords within your industry. A complete profile is a great way to increase your reach on LinkedIn.

2. Get active and remain that way: Having a LinkedIn account is not enough. You need to become active and use the account often. You can choose to follow others, invite others to follow you, read the blogs, and engage your followers. Other things you can do include joining groups, updating your status, and letting others know what you are up to.

3. Recommend and endorse others: While you want others to endorse and recommend you, you need to be doing the same on LinkedIn. When you recommend others, you will stand out as an authority figure and earn the respect of your peers. You will also increase your activity on the platform which will, in turn, enhance your reach.

4. Invite people from your official email address: An easy way of getting more followers is to search for people you already know on LinkedIn and inviting those that are not members. LinkedIn has a feature that helps you to achieve this quite easily.

5. Post and share content: If you want to increase your reach on LinkedIn, then you need to come up with great content and share it on the platform. The content can be a blog or article or any other relevant type. Ensure that the information provided is beneficial to professionals on the platform and make sure you use relevant keywords.

The Lifestyle Business

If you have a lifestyle that you are used to, then you can always make a business out of it. A lifestyle business can be started so as to help fund your lifestyle. Your business can be online, but the main aim will be to promote your lifestyle and benefit financially from it.

Such businesses are typically started with little or no financial resources. There are also no shareholders, no external partners, no bank loans and no venture capital. This leaves the owner with a lot of control over the business. The owner can also choose how fast or slow they want the business to grow.

Lifestyle businesses generally last many years especially compared to other types of businesses. These include an e-commerce store, a bed and breakfast, consultancy services, and blogging or writing. One of the benefits that you will enjoy operating a lifestyle business is the freedom of time. You will be free to choose when to work and when to do whatever you desire.

You also get to enjoy the choice of location. There are no requirements regarding the location and as the boss, you get to operate your lifestyle business from any location that you like. Another benefit that you stand to enjoy is financial freedom. You have the freedom to determine how large or fast you want your business to grow. In return, you get to determine your paycheck as well as income.

Tools, apps, software to manage and increase your reach on Linked

LinkedIn has become *the* social networking website for business executives, professionals, and business owners. It has also become a central hub for business to business selling. Recent statistics indicate that LinkedIn now has over 500 million members and over 80% of B2B selling originates here. To be successful on this social networking website, you need to increase your reach and manage the account appropriately. Here are some tools that can help enhance this.

1. Resume builder: LinkedIn has created a resume builder which you can use to turn your resume on the platform into an MS Word or PDF document. The process of doing so is very easy and fast and anyone can do it. Once you convert your LinkedIn resume into a PDF or MS Word document, you can then share it via Twitter, Facebook, LinkedIn, or to anyone on your email address. You can also edit, rearrange, print, and export details on the resume using the resume builder.

2. Rapportive: This app has been around for a couple of years and is great at supercharging your LinkedIn profile. It remains as effective today as it has always been. This tool is actually an extension of Chrome web browser and connects seamlessly with your Gmail account. Should you receive an email from a LinkedIn member, their profile will instantly appear in form of a summary so that you get a clear indication about the sender.

3. E-Link Pro: If you are looking to sell via LinkedIn, then one of the tools that you need to use is E-Link Pro. You first need to install this tool via your Chrome browser as an extension. Then you will develop a search queue of your target customers so they can be searched on LinkedIn. Once ready, just click on "Play" and E-Link Pro will begin the search. It will go through 800 different profiles searching for your target buyers. Most of these contacts will notice that you viewed their profiles. They will probably check you out and express an interest in what you are offering.

4. Hunter: This is an excellent tool that helps you locate the email address of anyone that you want. If you visit a profile and wish to find the email address of that member, then Hunter will track down the member's email and avail it.

5. Infinity: Infinity is a visualization tool for LinkedIn. It is used to showcase your professional network designed and built using Javascript APIs. All you need to do to get started is to log in by choosing "Sign in with LinkedIn." Once logged in, you can click then drag in order to zoom in and out, navigate through your contacts, and also search by status update, title, and name.

10 Mistakes People Make when Marketing on Social Media

By now, most business owners understand the need to advertise and market their businesses on social media. They have opened pages and accounts across different social media sites especially the major ones such as Facebook and Twitter. However, having a presence only is not sufficient. People still make mistakes on these social sites which cost them followers, leads, opportunities, and potential customers. Here are some mistakes that people make when marketing on social media.

1. Not posting regularly

There are people who open social media accounts and then forget about them. They probably think that having a presence on popular social media sites like Instagram and Facebook is enough. This is wrong and you will not attract any followers or customers. As a business owner, you should post content on a regular basis. Basically, you should post 4 or 5 times per week on Facebook and about 4 times per day for five days per week on Twitter.

2. Being on only one channel

Some people open an account or page on only one social media. They consider only that particular platform as important and the rest insignificant. This is wrong because you stand a better chance of success on multiple social media sites. Marketing across multiple social media sites is absolutely crucial for the success of your brand and business.

3. Dismissing social media marketing as ineffective:

Some people believe that social media is not suitable for their niche or industry. This is a common misconception where people believe that social media marketing is either for young people and millennials or for tech-savvy individuals. This is not true as the fastest growing demographic is people aged 45 to 54 on Facebook and those aged 55 to 65 years on Twitter. All other demographics are well represented too. Social media is very effective when it comes to marketing. Companies and businesses not using social media are losing out big time on the opportunities presented here.

4. Ignoring your followers

On many occasions, business owners with social media pages tend to ignore their followers. They think responding to comments or engaging in any other way with them is a waste of time. However, this is a grave mistake that will make your social media marketing efforts flounder. You followers may like your posts and content. If so they will leave comments, ask questions, and share your content with others. You need to get online and engage them. This is the best way to grow your account and gain new followers. Failure to do this will see your followers ignore your page and leave to follow your competitors.

5. Not dealing appropriately with negative social media feedback

All businesses fear negative feedback on social media. However, when this happens, an appropriate response is necessary. Such comments should not be ignored. Instead, any issues raised should be addressed, any necessary remedies should be offered, and an appropriate solution sought. Negative criticism should be viewed as an opportunity to improve and get things right. The person who left the comments should be politely approached and their specific issue addressed publicly if necessary so that all followers and audience see you actually taking action to remedy the situation.

6. Spamming

As much as it is important to post content and share with others, this should be done strategically and in moderation. Some people will use multiple links, numerous hashtags, and marketing messages with their content. Others keep reposting old posts and so on. This kind of spammy behavior is unacceptable and will annoy your followers.

7. Overly promoting yourself

Social networking websites are best for sharing, socializing, and communicating. Even as you have a marketing strategy and wish to promote your products and brand, you need to do so in moderation. Social media users have become averse to adverts and detest marketing and promotional content. They prefer to engage normally with brands. If you have to promote your business and brand, then do so subtly and tactfully.

8. Unreal followers

There are business owners who pay to have followers. However, paid followers are often not real followers. They may not be interested in your brand or industry. You will make very little headway with fake or unreal followers. Make sure that you grow your followers organically and within your industry. This way, you will receive followers that are genuinely interested in your products and your brand.

9. Posting poor quality content

As a business owner, you should post high-quality content that adds value to your followers' lives. All too often people will post average, low-quality posts that add little value to the lives of their social media followers. They will quickly start to ignore your page and posts altogether. This will be a disaster. You need to take time to come up with high-quality content that is memorable, intriguing, funny, and probably worth sharing.

10. Not having a well-thought-out plan

Before getting onto social media and opening a page for your business, you must think about your desires, ambitions, and goals. Take time and think about what you wish to achieve through your social media pages. Have a well-defined strategy and create a good plan. The plan should outline your budget, goals, and key performance indicators (KPI). This way, you will be able to achieve a lot more.

Chapter 6: Paid Advertising – Getting Paid Traffic

Businesses need to focus on marketing and advertising if they are to achieve growth, expansion, sales, and profits. The success of your business will largely be pegged on your marketing strategies and advertising is a major part of marketing. You should take time and come up with a successful marketing strategy that will see you achieve your ambitions.

What is paid advertising?

Paid advertising simply refers to advertising services that you have to pay for as compared to other forms such as earned advertising. Earned advertising may include word-of-mouth which you do not have to pay for.

Online advertising involves a lot of earned advertising. If you want success, sometimes you have to pay for it. There are different types of paid advertising. These include the following;

- Video ads
- Pay per click
- Pay per download
- Display ads
- Pay per view

Why are ads important?

One of the reasons why you should use advertising is that you get instant results. If you set up an ad, then you are likely to start receiving responses almost immediately. You will also start receiving increased traffic to your social media pages as well as your website. It is also an affordable yet effective way of bringing customers to your store.

The best place to start your advertising is on your chosen social media. Since Facebook is the largest social networking website with billions of followers. For this reason, it is advisable to begin your paid ads campaign here. You can then move to YouTube, Instagram, and Twitter. These four are among the best social media sites to begin your paid ads campaigns.

Ad Copies: An ad copy is the main text of a click advert. The ad copy has a number of elements including credibility, attention, the promise of a benefit, as well as a call to action.

Advertising also helps to keep your brand relevant. By regularly advertising, you will remain relevant in the eyes of your customers and social media followers.

Facebook

Facebook Ads have a micro-targeting feature. This feature allows you to reach the audience that you desire based on factors such as interests, location, and demographics.

Types of Facebook ads

- Photos ads
- Video ads
- Carousel ads
- Slideshow ads
- Instant ads

Cost of Facebook ads: The cost of Facebook ads varies depending on several factors. Daily amounts can be charged which will hardly exceed $11. If you choose to run your ad continuously, then expect to pay no more than $77 each week.

Instagram

Instagram ads are very similar to Facebook ads. There is no set amount for advertising and advertisers get to choose their own budgets. This gives you leeway to choose your preferred approach.

Cost of Instagram advertising: You should expect to pay anywhere from $0.20 to $2 for CPC or cost per click ads. You can opt for cost per mile ads which cost about $5 per 100 visitors.

Analytics: Instagram provides you with analytics. Focus only on merits that you can change. You should use the information obtained to improve your marketing.

Types of ads

- 30-second video ads
- Instagram marquee
- Multi-photo carousel ads
- Picture ads
- Interactive navigation

YouTube

YouTube ads are different from all others because YouTube is primarily a video sharing platform. There are several types of YouTube ads. These include;

- Display ads
- Bumper ads
- Skippable ads
- Non-skippable ads

Cost of YouTube ads: The cost of YouTube ads ranges from $0.10 to $0.30 for CPV or cost per view. You will pay $20 for your ad to reach 100,000 viewers.

Analytics: YouTube provides analytics for your videos. The analytics feature watch time reports, revenue reports, and interaction reports. You will want to focus on watch time views, the number of views, traffic sources, demographics, audience retention, and devices used to view your ads.

Twitter

Advertising on Twitter helps businesses to reach out to their followers, potential customers, and a target demographic. There are a number of different Twitter ads. These are;

- App card
- Lead generation card
- Photo card
- Gallery card
- Website card
- Player card

We also have;

- Promoted trends
- Promoted accounts
- Promoted tweets

Cost of Twitter Ads: The cost of a promoted tweet is $1.35 per engagement. Promoting a Twitter account costs between $2.50 and $4 per follower.

Twitter analytics: You should use analytics to find out the performance of your account and ads. There are some crucial statistics that you should pay attention to. These include the effectiveness of your ads and so on.

5 Mistakes People make when Advertising

1. Overdoing the ads

Sometimes we tend to create too many ads. This can cost a lot of money and may be spammy. Instead of overdoing the ads, you should spend your money on a few high quality extremely effective ads. Think about superior artworks and hire experts to help you prepare your ads.

2. Assuming that a business owner knows best

Sometimes we think that the business owner knows everything about the business, brands, and products. While this may be true, it is sometimes best to bring in an expert or outsider to prepare the advertisement. This way, you will get an objective view about the product and the right questions will be answered by the ad.

3. Making unsubstantiated claims

Advertisers sometimes make claims that they cannot substantiate. They often tend to say what customers want to hear and promising to solve all their problems. However, the product or brand may not be able to do everything claimed by the advertised. It is crucial to stick to the truth and not to make unsubstantiated claims.

4. Poor timing

It so often happens that advertisers place their ads at the wrong time. This happens especially when they place ads on Thursdays and Fridays just before people go shopping. This results in too many ads posted on these two days and the competition becomes extremely high. Placing ads on other days of the week could be just as effective but with less competition.

5. Targeting everyone

Advertisers fail when they try to target the entire market with their ads. They forget that niche markets are a lot more effective. It takes a lot more work and resources to post ads to the entire marketing. Targeted marketing within a niche or industry is a lot more effective yet costs less.

Conclusion

Social media marketing and advertising are essential for the success of small businesses. Numerous businesses have grown and thrived simply by capitalizing on opportunities found on social networking sites.

Major social networks such as Facebook, Twitter, Instagram, YouTube, Pinterest, and LinkedIn provide numerous opportunities to businesses of all sizes. This is because they have large numbers of users and most of these users are also consumers. Most consumers love to spend time on social media posting photos and socializing with their friends and families.

If you own a small business and wish to market your brand on social media, then you need to first determine which ones are the most relevant for your business. First, identify your customers and determine which social networks they are likely to be on.

Once you identify the right social networks, you should craft quality advertisements messages targeted at your specific industry. If you do this correctly, then you will benefit from the numerous opportunities offered by social networking websites. You will grow your following and increase your reach, acquire more customers, increase your sales, and also earn more profits.

Finally, if you found this book helpful, please leave a positive review on Amazon as it allows me to keep producing quality books.

www.ingramcontent.com/pod-product-compliance
Lightning Source LLC
Chambersburg PA
CBHW071503210326
41597CB00018B/2671